A+ Parenting

John Hitchcock

Published by John Hitchcock, 2022.

While every precaution has been taken in the preparation of this book, the publisher assumes no responsibility for errors or omissions, or for damages resulting from the use of the information contained herein.

A+ PARENTING

First edition. February 18, 2022.

ISBN: 979-8201165499

Written by John Hitchcock.

Table of Contents

Introduction

Who knew!

Parenting changes everything, doesn't it?

That softly crying babe in the delivery room now comes home from fourth grade with math homework... or maybe that little babe is now sixteen and still not back with the car he's driving for the first time.

Maybe it's the boys. They're always texting your daughter, asking her for help on homework, or so she says.

Speaking of homework, you are convinced if your child did it right, the grades would be higher than the "D" in biology.

The twenty-first century brings some unique difficulties into the process of raising good kids.

For Instance...

1. An abundance of EED's (Electronic Entertainment Devices)

2. Instant communication with friends by texting and cellphone

3. Communication with you decreasing

4. The trauma of being a single parent

5. TV and movies that constantly push the moral envelope

6. Increasing prevalence of ADD and ADHD

7. The continuing difficulty of undiagnosed dyslexia

It is not easy being a twenty-first century parent, but there are guiding principles that can help you get started or stay on the road to success and a good life for your child.

Chapter One - Focus on Hope

I have sworn upon the altar of God
eternal hostility against every form of
tyranny over the mind of man.
Thomas Jefferson

UPDATE: PARENTING AFTER THE PANDEMIC

We could see it coming

The results of a worldwide pandemic become personal when they have an obvious effect on our child. Hearing on the nightly news that students have lost a year of learning become real when we realize our child is having difficulty recognizing the meaning of words.

Being forced to leave our job to be at home for week after week of virtual learning as our child learned from a flat screen gave us a new perspective in how important learning simple tasks was.

Not only did we have to deal with the nuances of learning, but we saw other changes in our kids. Even if he was allowed to attend school, the mask mandates hid the brightness of smiles from his teacher or friends. Our children were growing up far removed from smiles and other facial expressions.

But it was more than masks. Not being able to play with their friends or be around other people began to take an emotional toll on our children. Loneliness became the norm or worse yet, developing a fear of being around others began to develop in our child. We knew this growing fear of other people was going to have long-term effects on our kids. Increasing amounts of depression and severe emotional problems also snuck into our lives.

Was fear the one common factor?

Our own fears, even if we thought we hid them well, may have had a profound influence on our kids. Our fears may have been more philosophical; being controlled by an overbearing government, having freedoms taken away, fear of out-of-control mandates, growing racial division... the list grows longer.

Even the fear of speaking up about our own beliefs became something to be dealt with.

Mixed-messaging from the "experts" created other fears. "Follow the science" became the mantra, but even that changed from day to day. Masking worked...but they didn't. Vaccines prevented Covid...but people still got infected. Mandates were serious enough to lose your job... but states without mandates were just like ours. China was the cause... or was it bats?

Such confusion created a widespread culture of fear, both among adults and children. That fear locked us into depression, anxiety, loneliness, anger, even the thought of suicide.

So What Can We Do?

The first step in combatting fear is to do something that enables us to show courage. Your willingness to take action that has risk requires you to put down fear. Believe me, the courage you show will encourage your kids and give them confidence in you as a parent. That "something" may be as simple as taking your children to a park for a play-date without masks. Maybe go for a visit to Grandparents or other family members.

There are other events which may really but your courage to a test.

1. Going to a School Board Meeting and voicing your opinion (whatever it may be) on Critical Race Theory.

2. Speaking to your neighbors about the need for keeping freedom prevalent in our country.
3. Going to school and asking to see if particular books are in the library.

There are other things you can do to give a sense of confidence to our kids?

1. Choose to do homeschooling full time.
2. Set a schedule for your children to do schoolwork.
3. Check your kids schoolwork each day.
4. Encourage your child to stand up and stand out for things that are right.
5. Teach your children there are things that are right and things that are wrong.
6. Monitor your child's social media.

Let's Address Root Causes!

I have to make a DISCLAIMER; What follows is NOT a racial or ethnicity issue. It is true right across the board!

There are three things that can help us be the best possible parents.

1. There is a father in the home.
2. Our kids are in a school that works.
3. We hold to the Truth that God exists and gives us strength to accomplish more that we can imagine.

Note: if you are a single Mom, you have my greatest praise. It's hard to keep a family going. Perhaps the best thing you can do is pay attention to number 3 in the list and find a church which may be able to offer help or assistance. Maybe even provide a surrogate father through youth groups or other youth-oriented activities. Perhaps even a man that will love you, marry and accept your kids as his own.

Honestly, we could write entire books on those three items. I suggest possible starting points could be as follows

1. Search YouTube for videos by Larry Elder and/or Candice Owens. Both strong proponents of a father in the home.
2. The same two people for how to fix schools. Thomas Sowell is another.
3. Find a good, Bible-teaching church in your neighborhood.

NOW ON WITH OUR ORIGINAL BOOK AND SOME GREAT IDEAS FOR PARENTING

We are all aware of the obvious... school should make sense and be a successful experience for your child.

It doesn't take a brilliant mind to understand that principle, but we sometimes forget exactly what it is that makes school success possible for your child.

Finally, with over fifty years of teaching science in both high school and college, I think I'm beginning to get it. The "it" I'm starting to understand has several important concepts, and I'd like to share some of them with you.

First, your child's success in school goes far beyond the grade they achieve in any particular class or how well they do on the infamous standardized exams. Doing well with grades or on standardized tests is a **byproduct** of students choosing to follow the pursuit of a concept that I call HOPE.

In this case, HOPE is an acronym meaning "**Higher Order Principles of Education.**"

Simply stated, it is important to live by those Higher Order Principles of Education. That means choosing to live by actively applying normal, traditional values to whatever you do.

The Journey Towards Radical Excellence.

If your children make a focused effort towards living their lives within the context of those Higher Order Principles, they will ultimately produce a life that excitingly illustrates a high level of Radical Excellence.

Some of those "traditional values" are listed here.

1. Responsibility
2. Enthusiasm
3. Integrity
4. Curiosity
5. Politeness
6. Timeliness
7. Commitment
8. Politeness

The danger in saying those things is that people will think, "Well of course! We all know that."

Most of us DO know those things, but here's a disturbing fact.

EED's... the roadblock to success.

More and more in our schools, public or private, a growing number of students have become enjoyably engrossed in their use of Electronic Enjoyment Devices like iPods and cell phones to the extent that they are forgetting (or ignoring) the productive application of those excellence-producing characteristics.

Saying something and actually doing that thing is what makes a hoped for success possible.

Having stated those principles used in producing excellent achievement, I would be guilty of a great omission if I didn't give you a **very practical example** of a specific activity you can do that will help your child in school.

Ask the right questions.

A typical dinner time conversation with your teenage child might sound like this.

"How was school today?"

"OK."

"Is all your homework done?"

"Yeah."

You might be amazed at the dialogue that could develop simply by changing the way you ask questions of your child. Let me give you a few examples.

"What was the funniest thing any of your teachers said today?"

"What questions did you ask in class today?"

"Which of your friends was the most enjoyable to be around?"

"Did you observe any acts of random kindness?"

"Let's study those vocabulary terms right after dinner, ok?"

"How did your math teacher help you see where math is used in everyday life?"

At the beginning of each school year we hear multitudes of inspirational words about how "We're all in this together."

Well, the fact is, we ARE in it together.

Let's see if we can make it work.

Chapter Two - The Blame Game

You can get discouraged many times,
but you are not a failure
until you begin to blame somebody else and stop trying."
John Burroughs

There are times when life isn't any fun.

The problem times of life can arise from an abundance of reasons, and when we are dealing with those times, we tend to place blame on someone else or some remote situation.

Whose fault is it?

The all pervasive and undefined *society* is always an easy target.

Reading the morning paper or seeing the news headlines online frequently creates the response, "What is our society coming to, anyway?"

Blaming society seemingly absolves us from personal involvement in a stressful situation. If society is the fundamental cause of the problems we face, who are we to think it possible to stand up and personally attack a problem?

Next in line to take the brunt of determining what causes a child's poor performance at school is the *neighborhood*. Where you live might not be the best place in the world, and certainly there are deficiencies that could have great influence on your kids. Significant poverty, an abundance of gang-bangers and massive unemployment are all major factors that do affect how we live.

On the other hand, you and your family can become victorious over anything if you go about it in the right way. You need to be strong. Be patient. Dig deep and develop the courage to become victors over tough circumstances.

The electronic universe.

I call them EED's (*Electronic Enjoyment Devices*), and the all-encompassing presence of smart phones, video games and computers is another focus where we can place blame for the shortcomings of our children. When you see thousands of text messages per month on your phone bill, maybe it's time to quit blaming the device. Rather than the device, the real problem resides with the decision-making ability of your child.

When the school report card comes home with two D's and one F and the rest C's, you may hear the common lament, "Everybody's doing poorly in those classes. The teachers really don't care about us and are not good at all."

Understand one simple fact when you hear the phrase "everybody's doing poorly" being translated usually means, "my three friends and I have the lowest grades in the class."

If you aren't perceptive and persistent, it is easy to fall into the trap of blaming *teachers* for your child's poor academic performance. There are times when your child may actually have a poor teacher, but almost always there are flaws in the daily routine of the student that result in their poor performance.

If it isn't teachers, the negatives in your child can always be blamed on their *friends*. If they only hung out with better kids, they would have better habits and thus do better in school. Peer pressure is a genuinely strong factor that has an effect on the habits and attitudes of our children. That pressure can be positive, but mostly seems to dwell on the negative.

As parents, we can quickly fall into the syndrome of blaming *drugs* for the poor performance of our children. The insidious danger of drugs cannot be ignored, but we must never fall into the trap of ascribing blame for the failings of our children on drugs alone. This concept will be discussed more thoroughly in a later chapter.

Blame might not be the cause.

All of the above reasons for blaming the factors that create deficiencies in our children might hide the real cause of their problems. This may be a hard thing to face, but the root of their problems might reside in the way your parenting has progressed... or not progressed.

As you continue through this book, I will suggest some very practical steps you can take that can result in improving the performance of your child in school. And as success in school becomes more apparent, the likelihood of success in other parts of their lives will increase.

For starters, you need to understand the starting point is realizing **The Mind Matters Most**. Every action, every decision starts with our minds. Everything we do is determined by what we think in our minds. From the smallest, most inconsequential items to major life-changing decisions, what we think in our mind ultimately determines the decisions we make.

Understand this. The decisions you make are yours. You need to own them, to take responsibility for the decision and the consequences of that decision.

Equally important, your children make their own decisions. You may try desperately to influence those decisions, but ultimately, they are the one who decide the actions that affect their lives.

Knowing this, there is only one logical conclusion.

Good parenting must focus on teaching our kids how to make wise decisions.

Chapter Three - Enable or Empower?

It's not what happens to you,
but how you react to it that matters.

Epictetus

Just like there are no perfect parents, there are no perfect kids. Plan on it. Your perfect angel will get in trouble, whether at home or in school.

Dealing with imperfection.

When problems happen, how are you going to react? Will you be the parent who automatically sticks up for your child who would "never do that?" Will you be the great enabler, doing everything possible to make the problem go away?

Or will you choose to be the wise parent who tells their child, "You deserve the consequences you are facing. We won't help get you out of the problem, but we will help you through it."

That is an excellent support system. When you acknowledge the wrong, but provide the support to help your child survive and grow, you are teaching positive lessons rather than simply inflicting punishment.

Simply put... get it on - get it done - get over it.

Done properly, there are times where "enabling" is an acceptable alternative. Done poorly, however, the enabling situation can have detrimental effects. For instance, some teachers offer extra credit. Some students who ask for that extra credit are really asking for "bail me out" credit since they haven't done their part. Wise teachers can offer a form of credit recovery that still forces the student to suffer some degree of consequence.

Extra credit that fails to provide realistic consequences does little to help the student stay in touch with the reality of responsibility. One of the most absurd instances I have seen was the student whose grade went from an "F" to passing by accomplishing the "extra credit" of not shaving for the month of November. Somehow that doesn't seem to meet the criteria of turning the situation into a positive, learning situation.

Identify the real problem.

Enabling a student can also hide the real problem. If a poor grade in school is caused by a student being disorganized, but the fixing is accomplished by giving a re-test, nothing much is accomplished except teaching the student there is always a way out of the problem. The more appropriate "consequence" might be letting the grade stand, then teaching your child better organizational skills.

I had a student who received an "F" on a lab report because all the physics was totally wrong. His father called me, rather adamant that the failing grade was unfair because the student had "worked really hard." The father thought it entirely appropriate that hard work was far more important than correct performance on any graded event. The irony of that argument became apparent when I reminded the man that his clients (he was a contractor) would not likely be content with working hard if the roof he installed fell down after the first month.

I do understand why parents want to reward their children for "working hard," but it is much better to couple that positive life-attribute with the production of quality, not necessarily perfect, work.

Perhaps the worst of all situations for enabling to occur is in the realm of cheating. None of us want to think our child would ever do such a thing, but the hard reality is that every kid is capable of giving in to that temptation. In those types of situations, no matter what the consequences, remember the bigger lesson of learning integrity far transcends any grade penalty the child might receive.

What about cheating?

High tech cheating has expanded the base of participants, and your child can become part of a cheating situation, even without the intent to do so. All it takes is one cheater with a cellphone and the contents of an exam can be known throughout their friends in the electronic universe.

All passengers in a car are guilty when one rider lights up a joint. The same is true and the guilt shared when the contents of a pilfered exam are sent out electronically.

School administrators have almost no choice but to count all recipients of a compromised exam guilty. Thus, a punishment could be applied to a large group of "friends," and your son or daughter could be included, even if they never used the material.

Your child will undoubtedly deny any involvement, and will most likely deny or defend the person who initiated the action. The "I would never rat on a friend" syndrome is very real, even if it is misdirected.

Never mentioning the event makes some degree of guilt a strong likelihood. When that happens, the proper thing to do is support whatever consequences the administrators propose – within reason.

The lesson learned here is to choose friends wisely and then inform someone, even parents, when inappropriate actions are occurring.

If your child is part of the cheating, it might also be a time to impose your own consequences in addition to those applied by the school. The school's punishment is for the cheating. Yours' is the violation of trust and integrity your child showed towards the family.

Chapter Four - Reward or Punish?

*If people are good only because they fear punishment,
and hope for reward, then we are a sorry lot indeed.*
Albert Einstein

The student was quite irate when she approached my desk.

"You just cost me two-hundred dollars!" were her opening words.

She went on to explain in a rather animated and angry way that because I GAVE her a C in chemistry, the money her parents had promised for getting nothing less than a B was gone.

My explaining that her average was right in the middle of the "C" range did little to calm her spirit. Neither did she feel better when I indicated how proud I was that she had raised her first semester grade from a "D" to the "C."

After she calmed down, and the realization that I was not going to raise her grade set in, we began discussing some negotiation options with her parents. Interestingly, when she returned to school the next day, she was fairly satisfied that they understood the improvement was significant, and they had taken her suggestion to keep on trying for the "B," and to lower the reward to one-hundred-fifty dollars.

I have mixed feelings on the use of rewards of that magnitude for getting arbitrary grades in classes. It can illustrate the good news - bad news syndrome. It can be good news if it actually works, but it can be bad news if the child begins to believe that life is always like this.

The totally opposite approach can produce similar conflicts.

I have seen students be grounded for a month, had their car keys locked up or, worse yet, had their cellphone confiscated for getting less than acceptable grades.

Every student and family situation is different. Even children in the same family need to be treated differently at times. I admit to having mixed reactions to this style of reward or punishment. As a self-confessed idealist, I like emphasizing the Higher Order reasons for learning take predominance over artificial rewards or punishment. Combining artificial grades to extrinsic rewards or punishment could dilute the learning and development of effective systems of doing the right thing in the right way.

One way of producing an effective compromise might be for the parent to give a partial reward for following a good system (i.e. doing the homework on time) while also rewarding the actual result.

Being a parent has never been easy. And today, I believe it has never been harder. Never has it been more critical to establish open lines of communication with your kids.

Start early, never give up. Your kids are your legacy. Make it good.

Chapter Five - Reading Really Works

You don't have to burn books to destroy a culture.
just get people to stop reading them.
Ray Bradbury
The more that you read, the more things you will know.
The more that you learn, the more places you'll go.
Dr. Seuss, *I Can Read With My Eyes Shut!*

Even in this digital video age, reading is still the fundamental skill that we all need. And we are not talking the banal travesty we call texting, either. Genuine reading, whether for enjoyment or information, is an absolute necessity.

As a parent who wants your child to succeed, there are several undeniably important facts you must comprehend and illustrate. Some of them might be things you already know. Other could be ides worth trying as you help your child achieve real academic success.

Success will be more likely for your child if they see you modeling the joy and functionality of reading. Kids do emulate their parents, and it is way more functional to say "Here, try doing this. It works for me." than to tell them to do something that you NEVER do.

Another critical component is to start the process early. Early in their lives, during those pre-bedtime snuggle moments, start with a colorful picture book. The sound of your voice, the warmth of your hugs and the presence of a book create a positive environment that gives confidence and joy to your child.

I said it early, but it needs repeating. You absolutely must be convinced that the ability to read for enjoyment and understanding is one of the most critical components of success in almost all endeavors of life. It cannot be ignored. It must be pursued.

You likely have already provided your child with their own cellphone. Serious consideration should be given to making their own ebook reader available. I still enjoy the tactile comfort of a traditional book, but the ownership of a reading device of their own emphasizes the importance of reading.

A positive family atmosphere can occur that emphasizes good reading by all reading the same novel, then sharing reactions and comments about it while eating the evening meal together.

You heard that right, didn't you?

Eating the evening meal TOGETHER! That is becoming a lost tradition, but I am convinced of the long-term benefit of sharing time and nutrition as a family. That concept will be discussed in a later chapter.

Family reading does not need to be formalized, but by selected discussions, it is possible to develop useful academic skills necessary for school success.

Thinking, analyzing, comparing and summarizing can all be emphasized by appropriate questioning and discussing?

Start early, stay the course, and think of the joy you will have as a grandparent discussing great books with your kids.

Chapter Six - Safe Surfing

*The Internet is so big, so powerful and pointless
that for some people it is a complete substitute for life*
Andrew Brown

Surfing the web is potentially more dangerous than riding a monster wave off the California coast. Who knows what evil lurks in that electronic abyss so easily accessed by our smart devices. The real danger of sexual predators or identity thieves can ruin lives in a moment.

Equally dangerous is the mental dullness and insensitivity to reality that can develop as your children live in this virtual world of weird videos and imagined demons. It is highly unlikely that unlimited texting or tweeting produces well thought out writing or discussion of deeply philosophical ideas.

The oxymoronic nature of the Internet is that with all its detractions and potential evils, there has never existed a medium more conducive to in-depth research, highly creative products and even the potential to provide service to others and profit to individuals.

There is a real battle in progress as the easy entertainment duels with the productive potential of the Internet and our amazingly brilliant machines. Unfortunately, as the machines tend to get "smarter," the users can become dumber.

It is our job as parents to help guide our kids on a path to develop the desire and skills in using what is at their fingertips for an ally rather than a destructive force. We need to show them that the Internet is more than online games and that research is more than an online encyclopedia.

Positive Practical Protections

There are some simple actions you can do to help keep your kids safe and focused.

1. Install a content blocker on computers used by your kids.

2. Check the history of their computer use frequently.

3. Place the family computer in a visible location.

4. Establish a limit on the number of texts sent per month.

5. Become a "friend" on your child's social networks.

6. Check the History of the computer after use

7. Set a limit on the number of texts per month

8. Check your data use bill and see if texts were sent when your child should have been in class

9. Determine the amount of time spent texting per month then require an equivalent amount of time be spent reading

Some Positive Family Actions

It is not all negative, and there are many positive things you can do as a family in using the Internet.

1. Access some online thinking games like chess or word games

2. Make some family videos and upload them to YouTube

3. Build a computer controlled robot

4. Learn how to use "voice to text" for writing school papers

5. Learn how to write and publish an ebook together

6. Start a family Internet business

7. Learn how to do geocaching... then do it.

8. Start a family blog

Nothing Happens by Accident

Everything is a choice. Remember, the mind matters most.

Left to their own decision making process, it seems that most kids will somehow tend to make negative decisions. Your role as a parent is to model wise choices in your own personal use of modern technology and guide, even control, the use of your children.

Just as proper driving technique is a learned and developed skill, the same is true of computer use. Left on their own to become adept at driving a car, you can expect a wreck from your child. Do all you can to prevent a mental or emotional wreck in the world of using the Internet or cellphones.

Chapter Seven - The Risk of Trying

I can accept failure,
everyone fails at something.
But I can't accept not trying.
Michael Jordan

A growing syndrome in classrooms is the student who sits in class and does nothing except breathe and grow older. And nothing means exactly that... nothing! Often the same is true for that student in other situations; watching TV, playing video games and doing nothing productive towards school or building a better life.

The results are obvious.

Do nothing - get terrible grades.

When exams or papers are returned, the response is still nothing. No overt sign of disappointment or positive resolve is apparent, just a continuing attitude of nothing.

In my opinion, there is an underlying event occurring. If a student doesn't do homework, never studies and is only consistent in doing nothing, there is automatically a possible response.

"If I had studied, I would have passed." is their inner response to terrible grades.

By not studying, the student can hold firmly to the false optimism of, "If only..."

If they DO study, and still get a bad grade, their poor performance become internally personal and they are forced to confront other issues.

This syndrome may have been initiated by poor prior performance that was never addressed or cured.

Start trying. It might actually work.

If you sense your child might be slipping into this attitude of nothingness, or is already there, you can take definitive action to reverse the trend.

1. Understand the problem will not be solved immediately.

2. Time management skills may need to be improved.

3. You may have to impose some parent-induced homework times.

4. Perhaps your child is overwhelmed by disorganization and needs your help getting reorganized.

5. Sometimes a tutor can provide the incentive to start trying again.

This will not cure itself.

Unfortunately, this type of activity (or inactivity) seldom fixes itself. It is a self-perpetuating syndrome that becomes addictive, and can lead to forms of depression. The student who is doing nothing wishes internally for the energy and ambition to try and do the right thing, but is unable to generate the incentive to change.

That is where you as a parent enter the picture. It may require highly directive action or, depending on the actual circumstances, more of a gentle, counseling approach.

Speaking of counseling, there are times where extreme inaction or withdrawal of energy may be the result of some type of trauma in the child's life. Divorce, drugs or the death of a family member or friend can trigger emotions and feelings that prevent the person from performing as they know they should.

Be alert to your child. You need to have the wisdom to take action when and where it is obviously needed.

Chapter Eight - Count Your Pills

I think if you were Satan and you were setting around
Trying to think up something that would just bring the human
race to its knees
What you would probably come up with is narcotics.
Cormac McCarthy, *No Country for Old Men*

With significant drug use now starting as early as middle school, it is critical that you are aware of the symptoms of drug use. Those symptoms can appear as normal middle school changes or activities, but you should be alert to what might be going on in your child's life.

Some symptoms of marijuana use.

Marijuana is readily available in almost any neighborhood or school. Its use can affect behavior and there are also some physical signs of its use.

Noticeable changes in behavior

1. Marijuana users often become unmotivated, even giving up activities that once greatly enthused them.

2. Participation in sports, music or other groups might decline or stop altogether.

3. School grades may start a slow, or sometimes rapid, decline.

4. Participating in family activities may become a low priority.

5. A sudden change in your child's peer group could happen.

6. Lack of concern in appearance or personal hygiene could occur as the use of marijuana increases.

7. Sometimes a depression type of behavior will occur. Your child might just describe it as being "mello" or "just chillin," but you know better.

7. Some marijuana users become abusive or argumentative.

Physical Signs of Marijuana Use.

Marijuana use, unlike alcohol, where the signs of use are often overt and overwhelming, is not always easy to detect. There are some physical signs that should make you suspicious that your child might be using marijuana. often with such simple remedies as a quick shower or a few drops of Visine.

1. Bloodshot eyes

2. Slow or slurred speech

3. Unwilling to make eye contact or unable to maintain an unsteady gaze

4. Taking showers at unusual times (to minimize the smell)

5. Unusual use of eye drops to clear bloodshot eyes.

Even though there is a strong push towards the legalization of marijuana, it is still considered by many to be a "gateway" drug to harder, more dangerous drugs. Please understand that legalization of marijuana will not lessen the potential dangers inherent in its use. You must continue to be vigilant and proactive in preventing your child from using marijuana either recreationally or as a reality escape.

Harder drugs can cause more extreme symptoms, some of which are listed below. Those listed come from the website http://drugs.ie/drugs_info/ and a more exhaustive list can be found on their site.

Important signs and symptoms of hard drug use.

General signs of drug use

There are some general signs to watch out for which may be linked to drug use. Bear in mind that all of the signs listed below could be caused by many reasons other than drug use such as puberty, social changes or medical conditions. Try not to jump to conclusions about drug use, as you may be wrong and isolate your teenager even more.

1. Secrecy about activities, slyness, caginess
2. Staying out unusually late
3. A lot of new friends, perhaps an older crowd
4. Lack of interest in old hobbies and activities
5. Memory loss
6. Mood swings – quite suddenly, may have fits of temper
7. Short attention span
8. Not taking care of their appearance
9. Wearing sunglasses to hide the effects of drugs on the eyes
10. Using deodorant or incense to hide the smell of drugs
11. Always being broke and trying to borrow money
12. Stealing from home or outside – money and stuff they can sell
13. Using slang terms for drugs
14. Social, personal and family relationships suffer
15. Poor work or school performance, may be skipping days
16. Losing appetite and weight
17. Becoming withdrawn and not wanting to talk

Amphetamines

You may notice some of the following but not everyone who uses this drug shows all these symptoms:

Hyperactivity

Jerky movements

Can't sleep
Very talkative
Grinding of teeth
Very large pupils
Sweating
Thirsty
No appetite
Staring
Comedown:
May cause depression, fear, listlessness, apathy, muscle aches, cramps, mood swings.

Benzodiazepines (sleeping tablets and tranquillizers)
Slurred speech
Gentle, monotone voice
Distracted
Calm
Agoraphobia – not wanting to leave the house
Reclusive – avoiding other people
Fear of people and going outside
Aggressive (when used with alcohol)
Passive (when used with opiates such as morphine and heroin)
Comedown: (after long time use):
May become even more reclusive, agoraphobic and scared of people, may behave more strangely, twitching eyes, tense neck

Cocaine
Similar to amphetamines (above) but also look out for:
Runny, itchy nose – due to snorting
Extremely rapid heartbeat
Comedown:

Unlike ecstasy and other amphetamines, in which the effects can last up to six hours, the rush of cocaine only lasts 2-3 minutes and the effects wear off in 12 - 13 minutes. The comedown effects are similar to amphetamines but are far more intense.

Ecstasy

You may notice some of the following but not everyone who uses this drug shows all these symptoms:

Hyperactivity

Unusual confidence

Jerky movements

Can't sleep

Very talkative

Grinding teeth

Very large pupils

Sweating

Thirsty

No appetite

Staring

'Spittin' cotton' – spit is like a cotton ball

Small folded square of paper in an envelope shape

Comedown:

May cause depression, fear, listlessness, apathy, muscle aches, cramps, mood swings.

Hash

Bloodshot eyes

Giggling (especially in when they first start using)

Distracted

Introverted

Short attention span

Going off on tangents, hard to follow their train of thought

Loss of short term memory – this will come back when they stop

'Bomb' burn on clothes – small burn marks caused by falling bits of ash

Torn off bits of cardboard from cigarette packets or other cardboard objects to make a roach' (a sort of filter)

Bits of loose cigarette tobacco around their room or in pockets

Butts of cigarettes with no stains on the filter

Cigarette papers such as Rizla and cigarettes together

Knives with burn marks from heating and inhaling hash smoke – 'hot knives'

Comedown:

May cause anxiety, restlessness

Heroin:

After a fix or after smoking heroin the person will be 'stoned'. Look out for:

Very small pupils

Light colored eyes turn bright blue

Eyes look glassy

'Goofing off' – looks like they are nodding off, hard to keep their eyes open

Unable to finish sentences

Slurred speech

Shallow breathing

Scratching

Excessive smoking

Loose facial muscles

Blood stains on clothes from using needles

Bloody tissues

'Track marks' – marks left by needles, especially on hands, arms and legs although any vein can be used

Burnt holes in furniture, bed linen or clothes caused by 'goofing' when smoking a cigarette

Burnt tin foil from smoking heroin – 'chasing the dragon'

Spoons going missing from the house, spoons with a blackened underside from 'cooking' heroin

Cut filters from cigarettes

Ties or laces in pockets – used as tourniquets to prepare the vein for injecting

Long sleeves in warm weather to hide track marks

Comedown:

Runny nose and eyes, excessive yawning, very large pupils

agitated, can't sleep, lack of energy, cranky, depressed

cold sweats or hot flushes, gooseflesh skin

overeating or under-eating,

severe diarrhea after constipation,

nausea, dry retching which produces bile

constant knot in stomach, severe cramps in stomach and back of legs

'the shakes' – spasms in arms and legs

violent spasms in the small of the back cause back to arch

panting, spontaneous orgasms in men and women

Check Your Medicine Cabinet

It is not easy being a parent. From all sides you are bombarded by messages from different groups; should you spank your child or not? Should Mom work or stay home? Attend public school or private. Couple those pressures with an increasing governmental involvement, and parenting successfully is becoming complicated.

There is one issue that is very straight forward. Or at least it should be.

Our kids should not be using drugs. But even in this issue there are levels of grayness.

For instance, some parents are either indifferent towards or blind about the misuse of prescription drugs by their children. In fact, some even think it is safe for a child to use a prescription drug not prescribed to them, either recreationally or for self-medicating illness or "not feeling well."

Ominous Findings

There are some scary findings from a study recently conducted by The Partnership at Drugfree.org that indicate an unexpected casual approach by many parents regarding the use and misuse of prescription drugs.

1. One in four teens has misused prescription drugs.

2. Prescription drug abuse has increased 33 percent since 2008.

3. Only 15 percent of parents talk to their children about misusing prescription drugs.

4. 20 percent of teens were under 14 years old when they first tried drugs.

5. The most commonly abused prescription drugs are Xanax, OxyContin and Vicodin.

6. Those drugs cause more deaths per year than heroin and cocaine combined.

7. Some parents and many kids think abusing prescription stimulants will help get good grades.

8. Almost one-third of parents believe that Ritalin and Adderall can help a child perform better academically.

9. One in four teens believes prescription drugs aid in study.

What steps can you take?

There are some proactive steps you can take to help your child make wise decisions about prescription drugs.

1. Talk with your child, starting early, about the dangers of prescription drugs.

2. Spend time with your child to keep their respect and to maintain good communication.

3. Keep close watch on your prescription medications and dispose of unused medications promptly and properly.

4. Model proper behavior about prescription drugs yourself.

Listen carefully to their words.

Just like other parts of their lives, there is a street-slang vocabulary used by teenagers when talking or texting about prescription drug use.

Xanax: Z-bar, Bricks, Benzos

Valium: Blues

Sedatives & Tranquilizers: Chill Pills, French Fries, Tranqs

Ritalin: Rid, Vitamin R, Jif, R-ball, Rittys, Rits

Adderall: Beans, Black Beauties, Christmas Trees, Double Trouble

Vicodin, OxyContin, Percocet and other Painkillers: Vike, Watson-387, Tuss, Big Boys, Cotton, OC, Cotton, Percs, Morph, Kicker

Even the parties and combinations of the misuse of prescription drugs have their own unique set of words. Your child could be talking about this right in front of you, and never be noticed unless you are aware of the types of slang being used.

1. Pharming

2. Pharm Parties

3. Recipe (mixing prescription drugs with alcoholic or other beverages)

4. Trail Mix (mixing various prescription drugs at pharm parties)

At Home Alcohol Abuse

One of the more subtle substance abuse areas for teens can be the in-home bar area. A small drink here, another there, and your child may be starting down the road towards dependence on alcohol.

If you do have a bar or wine cellar, it is wise to keep a close eye on the remaining amounts. If you have younger children who might not have the wisdom or knowledge to try small amounts, it may even be a good idea to keep your liquor cabinet locked. A small body and too much alcohol can be a deadly combination.

Another danger signal for the potential misuse of alcohol is if your 15 or 16 year old teen is suddenly hanging out with similar age friends, but with a 21-year old in the group. That is the one who could legally purchase the alcohol, then make it available to the group.

Amazingly, there are also parents who provide alcohol to underage teens when a party is being held at their home. Any rumors or allegations that you hear about such activities should wave a red flag boldly in your face, and should be totally investigated before letting your teen attend a party in such a place.

Find where to get help.

If your child is misusing any substances at all, you may find that eliminating the problem is beyond your personal ability to solve. In that case, it is your responsibility as a parent to seek outside help, whether professionally or not.

The most important issue here is to let go of the need for total privacy. It may be embarrassing or you may even feel like a parental failure, but the health and welfare of your child is more important than temporary discomfort on your part.

There are some logical first steps to take.

1. Perhaps you have friends who have gone through similar problems. Start there.

2. Counselors at your child's school might be able to provide insight.

3. Your church may have a support or intervention program.

4. It may be necessary to seek the help of professional substance abuse workers.

5. If extreme intervention is necessary, some sort of rehab or intervention may be required.

Start Early. Never Give Up.

This has been a long chapter, but substance abuse is a big problem. Often it is a problem we are blind to until it becomes extreme. It is also one we sometimes do not want to face.

"Not my child..." is a safety barrier many parents erect. They ignore the problem until their child is in serious, perhaps deadly, circumstances.

You are not infringing on your child's privacy if you are alert and proactive in keeping them free from substance abuse. Indeed, it is your responsibility to do so. That intervention or

investigation may create tense, even adversarial, moments. Those will not be enjoyable times, but the benefit will eventually overcome the distress of those times.

Do not ignore the obvious. Intervene. Seek help. Be successful.

Chapter Nine - Learn Their Language

I would make an anonymous call and say,
this is someone who cares,
do you know what kind of children you have?
Elizabeth Berg, *Joy School*

Words are important. So are the words hidden between the lines or shown in the body. And with the increasingly hidden life of many teenagers, the current meanings of words can carry disastrous messages.

It is not just the unique abbreviations used in texting (lol, bff, etc.) but the spoken words that convey a message expected to be hidden from parents and older people... meaning anyone over thirty.

For instance, the phrase, "go nike..." sends a message of sexual activity. As you remember, the Nike corporation had an advertising campaign that said, "just do it!" Many teens have taken that phrase, changed it to "go nike," meaning just do it... meaning let's have sex.

FWB is a shorthand notation meaning "Friends With Benefits." Those benefits can include a broad spectrum, but mostly focused on either sexual activity or drug use.

Kids are not stupid, but they think we are.

Any kid dumb enough to be talking on their cellphone in your presence and use the word marijuana or heroin is too dumb to not have been caught already. They will use one or more of the common street names for the various drugs.

For instance, if you hear the numbers 420 slipped into a conversation you can be sure they are not telling the time of the party. 420 is simply one of the more common street names for marijuana.

If you listen carefully to what your kids are saying, you might not have a clue what they are talking about. Teen slang is constantly changing, and some of the meanings of common sounding phrases would surprise, maybe even shock you.

Following is a short list of some of the more common slang terms.

1. *Chillin'* - Means relaxing.

2. *Dope* - Means cool or awesome.

3. *Fly* - Boys tend to refer to girls they think are good looking as 'fly'.

4. *Hater or h8er* - This refers to someone who hates everything.

5. *Hardcore* - Means something is intense, generally good, but not always so.

6. *My bad* - It means 'my mistake'.

7. *OMG* - An abbreviation for oh my gosh or oh my god!

8. *Sick*- This no longer means someone doesn't feel well. It is used to describe something or someone who is cool or awesome.

9. *Tight* - Means close in relationship, as in "Me and her are tight." Note the generally wrong use of pronouns by teens.

10. *Tool* - A person who is either stupid or a geek.

11. *Wanksta* - A person who trys to act tough, but isn't successful at it.

One of the most complete compilations of teen slang can be found at http://www.thesource4ym.com/SlangDictionary/SlangDictionary.aspx

Body language speaks louder than words.

When body language does not line up with the words your child is saying, you must use great wisdom in how you respond. You know what they say is definitely not the truth or what they really think, but almost always an adversarial response will only deepen the problem.

"Don't roll your eyes at me." might not be the best way to confront the message they are sending. Rather, you will be wise to incorporate their body language logically into the conversation.

Try a response like, "I know you are frustrated, but try and see it from my perspective, even a little bit." You may find that response will enable the conversation to continue in a more fruitful manner.

Chapter Ten - Know Their Friends

For in today's generation of teenagers
finding acceptance is hard,
especially for those who dare to be different-
then it's impossible.
Rebecah McManus, *Colliding Worlds*
Know Their Friends

Kids are impulsive. They jump first, think later.

We know wisdom arrives after experience, and the choice of friends our children make is a classic example. A vibrant and authoritative personality can suck our offspring into an intriguing relationship that can be either good, bad or really ugly.

Understand the importance of information.

Knowing who your child hangs out with is critical to their success and safety. The proper friends can have positive results, while choosing in a bad way can lead your child down a path that could take years, even a lifetime, to recover from.

You need to set the tone early that you need and want to know who their friends are, and what kind of people they happen to be. Parental responsibility mandates that you have that information, and, especially when your child is younger, can determine who their primary friends are.

It might not be comfortable, but keeping close track of your child's friends is important. There are some definitive actions you can do to give you the information needed. Most importantly, start early in the process and the intervention you are exerting will be natural and expected as your child grows into the teenage years.

1. If your house allows it, try and host parties and provide a place for small groups of friends to hang out together.

2. When that is not possible, make sure you know what the parents who are hosting are like. Do you have confidence the hosting parents would conduct the party in a way that makes you comfortable?

3. If your child says they are going to a party at a particular place, it is totally okay to make a call or visit just to make sure what you were told is actually happening.

4. There may be opportunity to ask your child's teachers or counselors what kind of friends your child has at school, and whether the teacher thinks they are wise choices.

One of the most effective actions you can take is to create positive opportunities for your child to make really good friends, but in situations you automatically have knowledge about.

1. Join an athletic team and participate as a family.

2. Find things your family and other friends with kids of similar age can do together.

Technological friends need checking, too.

In our keyboard connection world, you need to keep a close watch on your child's online and texting friends. Just as with the living and breathing friends, there are things you can do to help your child make proper decisions.

1. Always be a member of their social media adventures.

2. Make it a habit to check their smart phone address book.

3. Be sure you have passwords for email and other accounts your child uses.

4. Check the cellphone texting use. Make sure it lines up with what you see on their phone.

5. In extreme cases, you may find it necessary to install tracking devices on your automobile if used by your teenage driver.

This is the 21st Century!

Times are not like when you were a kid. Mostly, thing are better and enjoyment is more easily obtained. The nuclear family differs remarkably from what you experienced growing up. Technology has made "friendships" possible without ever meeting face-to-face... until a disaster could occur.

Thus, even though you may be uncomfortable and feel like you are spying on your kids, it has now become an acceptable and necessary component of parenting. So buck it up. Know your child... and his or her friends.

But my child has NO friends.

If your child has no friends and is a total "loaner," that could be indicative of a potentially dangerous situation. You may need to create situation in which interaction with others is possible. Chances are your child is uncomfortable with meeting new peers, and it then becomes your job as a parent to find safe situations in which friendships can be developed slowly and within the comfort level of your child.

You can do that by having your child join small, safe groups at church or community groups in which you also participate. Even participating in a 5k benefit walk can start the interacting with others.

On the negative side, if your son or daughter is friendless, that may be a symptom of a deeper problem. In that case, seeking the aid of a counselor or professional could be the wisest action you can take.

The parenting tightrope.

There are no real easy answers to the skill of raising good kids. The whole process requires the knowledge and wisdom to determine whether to intervene or not. You want to raise your children to be independent, yet to have responsibility and trustworthiness.

It seems that the earlier we start the more natural the entire process becomes. Intervening in the choices of a three-year-old is going to be less adversarial that when the child is fourteen. But those interventions and modeling occur at a young age will, more often than not, create confidence and growing wisdom in your teenage children.

Be strong, be patient. Be a great parent.

Chapter Eleven - Go Fly a Kite

*"I have always thought the actions of men
the best interpreters of their thoughts."*
John Locke

There is a big difference between having kids and raising kids. You want your children to be raised to become successful adults, having great families and being an effective person in serving others. The legacy you leave your children starts being built the first day they are in your home.

Kites and bikes.

I was doing the "Dad thing" by showing my son how to fly his first kite. As it floated skyward over the beaver dam next to the house, we were both excited as the string whirled off the ball attached to the stick I was holding.

A perfect breeze, a deep blue sky, the kite with its colorful tail flying beautifully... and disaster struck.

You know what? They do not tie that string to the end of the stick!

As the kite extended, the string zipping from the holder, when the end came the kite seemed to savor the new-found freedom and soared flauntingly into kite heaven.

I stood there with the empty stick, unable to say any comforting words as my six-year-old son's eyes sent the message, "Dad, what were you thinking?"

Parenting efforts gone awry were unleashed on our daughter even more profoundly.

The training wheels were off, and our daughter was getting comfortable on the two-wheeler for the first time. The first few rides were uneventful as she peddled optimistically, feeling the comfort of my stabilizing hand on the back of the seat.

Her first freedom ride started as we got her comfortably under motion down the slightly inclined driveway between the house and the barn. Once going with sufficient speed to maintain balance, I removed my hand and became the proud parent watching her first solo ride.

"Marla, stop, you're headed for the dump!" I shouted as the bike rapidly approached the embankment over which the farm dump existed.

"Oh, no! I didn't show her the brakes!" screamed in my head.

Fortunately there were no injuries sustained from her unintended trip into the dump. No injuries for her, but the "Dad, what were you thinking?" question, though unsaid, permeated the climate.

We laugh now, but those were some parenting episodes gone wrong. The event may not have been what was envisioned, but the moments meant more than the immediate disaster. Perhaps the lesson learned was that parenting involvement was more important than parent perfection.

High tech creates low action.

As we were talking about his high-tech toys, a student said to me, "Being a kid must have been boring to you without these things, wasn't it?" He followed that with, "What DID you do, anyway?"

My response was simple.

"Well, let's see... I helped in the farm chores, raised chickens and sold the eggs, went hunting, fishing, camping, skiing, bowling, played golf, built forts and snow caves, was an amateur radio operator, played baseball, had neighborhood softball games, tried playing trumpet, climbed mountains, read books and even went to school. Yeah, I guess you're right. Life must have been boring when I was a kid."

His enthusiasm dimmed as he said, "Wow! I get to hang out at the mall and go to movies. You were lucky."

You can overcome the easy electronic entertainment.

In retrospect, it is easier raising kids on a farm than in the heart of a city or engulfed by suburbia.

It might be harder where you are and in your unique circumstances. If you are a single parent, or if both parents work, it will be tougher to find the right activities for you to share with or make available to your children.

Nevertheless, there are a number of positive things you can do with or make available to your children.

Try participating in some of the following.

Go skiing

Take up bowling

Play table games

Go to museums

Attend a concert

Do creative photography together

Start doing geocaching

Go camping

Learn to play golf together

Sign up for an art class

Undertake a building project

Play tennis together

Have a family night out

Visit national or state parks

Learn a new language together

Create an Internet business together

Attend your child's school activities

Take your child to work one day

Go out to a diner for breakfast

Start a family blog

Kids often say they are bored. That is their choice. Help them get over it!

There is always hope.

Your situation may seem hopeless. You may think you have been victimized and are unable to be the kind of parent you know you children deserve. Do your best to overcome that attitude.

It will take work, some degree of creativity and quite a bit of patience.

But you can do it. One step at a time can help you become the kind of parent who produces a positive legacy in your family.

One practical activity that can reap long-term benefits is quite simple.

Make every possible effort to eat dinner together. Sit down, pass the potatoes and enjoy chatting with each other. Unfortunately, eating together is becoming a lost tradition.

When our son was in his graduate program, one professor assigned the class the task of remembering what life was like when they were six years old. The students were then asked to draw a picture of what dinner time looked like at their home.

Unbelievably, our son was the only person in a class of nineteen to draw a picture of the whole family sitting together at dinner. Everyone else had kids eating frozen dinner in their rooms, the mother watching TV with dinner in her lap and the father eating dinner out with business associates. Other options were presented, but the main idea was that being together was not part of the meal.

From a practical viewpoint, when you do eat together, whether at home or in a restaurant, make one inviolable rule... all cellphones OFF and all video games away.

Never, ever, give up being a great parent.

Chapter Twelve - Nuts & Bolts of School & Success

"In school we learn that mistakes are bad, and we are punished for making them.
Yet, if you look at the way humans are designed to learn, we learn by making mistakes. We learn to walk by falling down. If we never fell down, we would never walk."
— Robert T. Kiyosaki, *Rich Dad, Poor Dad*

Please note that this chapter is actually one included in another ebook I wrote entitled *Get a Grip – Join Life*. I am reproducing that chapter in this ebook because it contains specific attitudes and actions that students need to develop to make their time in school a success.

Pay attention to doing the right things.

Many students think the "stuff" they are supposed to learn in school is unnecessary and useless.

"When am I ever going to use this?" is the whining question constantly being asked.

"Maybe never." is the honest answer. But it is the honest answer to the wrong question.

The better question is, "How does what I learn in school help me live a better life?"

Believe it or not, there are people who live a very nice life, but can't tell you the name of the tenth president or how to solve the quadratic equation. What they can do, however, is benefit from the positive habits they learned and developed in school.

1. learning to listen intently
2. maintaining their responsibility

3. doing things on time

4. discovering how to think critically

5. doing uninteresting tasks well

The list could continue, but you get the idea.

Success trumps stuff.

The ultimate benefit of school is the level of success you achieve by learning how to do the right things at the right time in the right way.

Done properly, school can empower you with the following.

1. Learning how to perform with excellence without the need for enjoyment.

2. Discovering your best learning style.

3. Knowing how to adjust to different leadership (teaching) styles.

4. Developing character traits of persistence, patience, passion and integrity.

5. Building a strong resume of references, academics and extracurriculars.

You EARN the right to success.

Living in this age of entitlement we think that society "owes us" a personal level of success simply because we are a living, breathing person.

The Declaration of Independence says, "...."

Therefore, after the "...life, liberty and the PURSUIT of happiness..." we are pretty much on our own.

It is up to us to achieve or abdicate.

You will never reach your success potential if playing "Call of Duty" keeps you up till 3 AM or you indulge in whacky weed weekends on a regular basis. If your phone bill shows twenty thousand text messages per month, you might begin to think there is some wasted time there.

Nuts and Bolts of A's and B's.

There are some practical actions you can take to help assure you achieving a strong academic performance... even if you don't have a genius gene.

1. Procrastinate later.

2. Work first, play guilt free.

3. Find a smart spot to study or work. (personally, I like a donut shop)

4. Don't go overboard. Set a timer.

5. Choose friends who help, not hinder.

I have had the honor of interacting with almost six thousand students in my teaching career, and each one brings something unique to the big picture of being alive. May I share some of their stories with you?

Kids I have known.

Susan – 1970

Her tears traced glistening rivulets down sun-bronzed cheeks.

"Mr. H., I'm going to flunk physics." she sobbed.

"Susan, you're not flunking. Your average is almost 90." I tried to reassure her, surprised at the worry she appeared to have.

"You don't understand," she said almost in a whisper. "I'm choosing to flunk."

With that, amid sobs and tears, she explained how her friends had labeled her "snobby Susan" ever since the beginning of the semester when she had broken from the grasp of the general level classes to enter the college prep classes. Susan desperately wanted out and back in the classes with her friends, but her parents, knowing her ability, wouldn't let her drop from the college prep class.

Her parents wouldn't let her drop. Her friends wouldn't let her forget.

Susan finished the year with an average of sixty and accomplished her goal of failing the class.

Blake – 1984

Blake was trying to explain to me the mini-war that had created numerous clashes in the halls of our small town, rural school.

"It's the jocks against the nerds, Mr. H." he explained patiently, trying to justify why he was being suspended for two days as a consequence for beating up a classmate. Trying to elicit my understanding and also convince me why he shouldn't be penalized for missing chemistry, Blake's words were precisely formulated and well-spoken.

At two-hundred-twenty pounds, just over six-feet, and an impressive athletic presence as leading tackler on the football team, Blake also had a solid A-plus average in Advanced Placement chemistry. As captain of the football team he felt an obligation to lead in this brewing battle, even if the path down which he led wasn't exactly where he wanted to go.

Even in his stress as he sought my sympathy, Blake couldn't resist a chuckle as I finally asked, "Tell me, Blake, are you a jock or a nerd?"

Autobiographical – 1953

It was my first day in the big school. Seventh grade. Mrs. Monroe's morning homeroom.

Having spent my first six grades with ten other students in the one-room school up in Bakers Mills, I was marveling at twenty-six kids being in the same grade, much less the same room.

"Hi, my name's Tommy." One of the kids who sat right in front of me said. "I'm from the village." he said, indicating the big town of over one-thousand people where the central school was located.

"Where you from?" he asked.

"Up in Bakers Mills." I replied, thankful for his friendliness.

"Oh, Dog Town!" His tone changed as he referred to the nickname our town had acquired from the time in history when dogs did outnumber the fifty-nine residents.

"You must be stupid." he sneered. "Ain't nobody smart from Dog Town."

Stan – 1974

"You gotta be S*%##@'n me!" Stan's eyes brightened as he watched the smooth stream of water from the faucet being deflected almost ninety degrees by the negatively charged rod.

Stan lived on a farm, milked cows before coming to school in the morning, and somehow ended up in my general physics class. Physics fascinated Stan. He even spent time in my room after school learning algebra so he could solve the physics problems.

Stan was a "closet intellectual," hiding from his friends his interest in academic things.

"Why don't you go to college, Stan? Study physics. Be an engineer." I probed one day.

"Mr. H., I'd love to, but I'm gonna take over the farm when Pop retires." he replied. "That's what I'm s'posed to do."

The next fall, when Stan was a senior, his father had a stroke. Stan quit school to take over the farm. Two years later the farm sold at auction. Stan went to work as a farm hand for his neighbor.

Today Stan is married to his second wife, has seven kids, and still works on the neighbor's farm.

Kevin – 1997

Kevin had been suspended from school for smoking marijuana and was still under suspicion for dealing dope. Now back in school, he sat in the front of the room on the left side table. He sat with his druggie friends. Slouched down in the seats and seething with anger, all three played the part perfectly.

Except for one thing.

Kevin often hung back after class. Waiting till everyone was out of the room he would ask some question of science that had been mulling in his mind as he watched NOVA or Discovery Channel.

As the year continued an interesting syndrome surfaced.

Kevin would become intensely interested in a particular topic in class. He became quite vocal in class discussions, especially about general relativity and quantum physics. One day his body was leaning forward in total immersion in the topic. Suddenly, in a victorious moment of breaking away, Kevin picked up his books and moved to the empty table right in the middle front of the room.

Kevin still hangs with his buddies in the hall. But there's hope.

Unknown Students – 2006

I was leaving my room as first lunch began in the large public school where I recently taught.

A junior student was about forty feet away when he shouted to his friend walking up behind me.

"Hey, Dude, you seen Jason around? Don't he go here no more?" he inquired loudly.

"Din'ja here?" his friend shouted back. "He got hisself shot."

What identifies you?

Each of my students has their own story, their own identity. I have been fortunate to have known so many fine folk, learning something from almost all of them.

In this world of learning how to be successful in school and the rest of life, there are some important questions you should ask yourself.

(1) What do you envision your life to be like in three years?

(2) What steps are you taking today to be closer to that goal tomorrow?

(3) Do you want your own kids to become the kind of student you are today?

There you have it. School doesn't have to be fun like a video game or enjoyable like mountain biking. But it can be productive and functional, leading to a more successful and beneficial life for you and your friends.

Chapter Thirteen - Big Problems? Find Hope!

The solution to adult problems tomorrow
depends on large measure upon
how our children grow up today.
Margaret Mead

Everyone I know has problems. Life is like that.

Seriously, there is not a person that I know rather well who does not have some kind of issue that stays with them daily and usually throughout their entire life. The problem may change, but we all seem to carry something in our lives that can make our heart heavy.

Those problems can be of many different kinds.

1. Drugs
2. Divorce
3. Death
4. Disease
5. Disabilities
6. Disasters

Some problems jump into our lives through no fault of our own. The wildfire that destroys our home and possessions is not within our control, but can create massive difficulties.

An addiction to alcohol can be our choice, and the problems that follow are the result of personal decisions either to indulge in momentary pleasure or fail to seek professional help.

In either case, it is likely that you or your children have something that must be dealt with on a daily basis. Life is not always easy, and the normal problems of being alive can make good parenting even harder to attain.

Deal with it.

It almost sounds harsh, but when facing those seemingly impossible problems, we need to make the choice of confronting the ongoing problem in a way that the rest of our life is disrupted as little as possible. Those choices are not always easy, but they are choices.

Our mind matters most, and the attitude we choose to adopt will affect the entirety of our life.

For instance, one of my friends lost an arm in a farm accident when he was a young child. Rather than bemoan his fate and stand on the sidelines of life, he chose to deal with his loss as simply a modification of some normal activities.

He became a pastor, built buildings, repaired cars, built grandfather clocks as a hobby and was an excellent pitcher and hitter on our softball team.

His problem was always there, but his mindset transcended sympathy and depression.

Defeat depression.

When your problem becomes your passion, the risk of depression sneaks into your life. Emotionally healthy people are not immune from problems. They deal with them in a way that either solves the problem or makes it bearable. Even if the problem continues to exist, they acknowledge it, but put it in such a perspective that the rest of their life continues in a normal and productive manner.

Strong emotional and mental courage enables you to confront a problem appropriately, yet not be consumed to the point of defeat. You do not have to pretend the problem does not exist; you simply have to keep it in a place where you continue to function properly in the rest of life.

That is not always easy, and you may find the need for some strong friendship support or even professional counseling, but it is possible.

Be patient, be strong. Overcome.

What does this have to do with grades?

Whether you are the one with significant problems, or your child is the one dealing with these things that can upset normal living, the approach you take to the problems has a significant effect on the level of success (or failure) in the normal activities of life, school included.

Perhaps your teenager did something really stupid and is in trouble with the law. Court cases are coming, perhaps even juvenile detention or problems you face for not controlling your child.

You and your child have a problem. A big one. And one that is going to change some things in your life.

Yet life still happens. There is a long way to go. There is even tomorrow to deal with.

You face serious decisions in how to deal with the situation, and those decisions are going to impact the actions and relationship between you and your child for the rest of life.

Are you going to defend those stupid teenage actions or give strong emotional and physical support as your child deals with the consequences?

The memories and realities of that problem will be continuing, but there are other areas of life that need to be completed successfully.

Preventive Parenting.

You are the parent, you kid is the child. That simple fact gives you the right, indeed, the obligation, to intervene in creating proper behavior and diminishing actions that you know to be detrimental.

Bill Cosby, the comedian and activist, summed it up nicely when he said, "Kids are like homeless people - no job, no responsibility, and no house."

They are living in your house, supported by your income, thus are your responsibility. And you have every right to raise them in the proper way.

Too much TV? Turn it off.

Video games all night? Confiscate the equipment.

Caught "sexting?" Goodbye smartphone.

Have you had "The Talk?"

Speaking of sexting and big problems, there is one stupid decision that inevitably has life-long ramifications.

Two teens, one boy one girl, at home alone or out on a secluded date... and the pregnancy happens.

Now what?

Chances are the guy disappears into the oblivion of wherever teenage boys go after becoming a baby daddy. The girl now has the big questions to face.

Is abortion an option, with the likely life-long guilt or wondering that will follow?

Should the child be put up for adoption?

What about raising the child as a single, teenage mother?

Even if the boy stays around, questions of marriage or living together, maybe even with Mom and Dad arise.

Obviously, a new set of problems that radically change lives are now on the scene.

This is one of those issues where "The Talk" becomes crucial. There is no magical right time to address this issue, but one principle is generally quite appropriate. When your child, even at a young age, asks a good leading question, NOW is the time to give an answer appropriate to their age level.

Chances are pretty good that as the child gets older the questions become more specific. Each time your response can expand into the reality of the wisdom of waiting for marriage for sexual relationships.

Chapter Fourteen - Got God?

Even youths grow tired and weary,
and young men stumble and fall;
but those who hope in the LORD
will renew their strength.
They will soar on wings like eagles;
they will run and not grow weary,
they will walk and not be faint.

Isaiah 40:30-31

In our increasingly secularized world, this topic is considered off limits. It may be off limits, but is the most critical choice you make as a parent.

There are two choices in life we make, either purposefully or by acquiescence. God either exists or He does not. "Maybe" is not a choice.

God is not a reality TV program.

You may wonder, you may question, even doubt. In any case, your questioning or doubt does not change the reality. He is or He isn't.

Our belief or non-belief is NOT what determines His existence, no more or less than our "belief" in the reality of the Grand Canyon. It is there, no matter what we believe about it.

I have chosen to base my living on the acceptance of the real existence of God. There are two strong indications that the reality of God is a logical fact.

The universe, from the infinite to the infinitesimal, cries out beauty and chaos, both bundled into a complex entity that actually works. Random chance intermolecular interactions could never produce the overwhelming diversity and beauty of the life forms we observe. An Intelligent Designer is stamped throughout the universe, from the beauty of the heavens to the intricate functioning at the atomic level and below.

Second, God actually gave us the story of life and how it should be lived in His Word, the Bible. From the creation story through the history of humans and the end of times, the Bible makes sense of the meaning in lie and the hope of eternity.

A pyramid of priorities.

Reading the Bible leads logically to an ordering of life that creates a well-lived existence, for individuals and society at large. This arrangement seemed logical to me as I formulated my answer to a question one of my students asked.

"Your enthusiasm in class makes me think chemistry must be the most important thing in your life. Is that true?" was his intriguing question.

After thinking a moment, my answer followed. Not hardly. Let me share my priorities ahead of chemistry... and even physics."

I then relayed the following order of priorities.

1. My relationship with God.
2. My relationship with my spouse.
3. My relationship with my kids and grandkids.
4. My relationship with my parents.
5. My relationship with my at-large family.
6. My relationship with my close friends.

7. My decisions about how I treat all people and can be of service.

8. My decisions about how I spend my free and recreational time.

9. My attitude and enthusiasm towards my career.

10. Everything else.

I do not always hold fast to those priorities because there are times where one moves higher or lower as the need arises. But in general, focusing our energies in that order results in a healthy and rewarding life.

Meaning, purpose and passion.

There is an intrinsic need to sense a real meaning to life.

Why do we exist?

What's the point?

Am I important?

What happens after death?

Who cares if I live or die?

Those are tough questions that cry loudly for an answer.

When you think logically about the possible answers, it becomes necessary to start at the beginning. If we are simply the result of random molecular rearrangement over millions of years, how deep can that meaning go?

Conversely, if there is a Higher Order Being, perhaps there is purpose in us being here. Just maybe our actions and attitudes count for something beyond our individual, selfish enjoyment.

If we choose the latter option, it can give us a growing passion to live life in a way that unleashes our purpose. And when we couple that purpose with passion, life becomes good and our legacy enduring.

As a person, choose wisely.

As a parent, teach wisely.

***

About the Author

Once I understood you don't have to be perfect to be successful, life became enjoyable. My parents taught me that doing the right thing at the right time produced positive results.

Mom and Dad both worked, but that did not prevent us from doing things as a family. We went camping, played neighborhood softball games, went to the drive-in theater for all the John Wayne movies, bowled together, and ate dinner (actually, we called it supper) together.

My independent actions and ideas were allowed, even encouraged. Buying amateur radio equipment or a new BB-gun gave me the opportunity to find a job to pay for it. Thus, raising chickens and selling the eggs, even picking and canning tomatoes for the lady down the road became part of my middle school years.

During the early years of college, my relationship with God gave me the courage to deal with some tough emotional challenges.

Now, as an experienced classroom teacher, parent and grandparent, I am thankful for the parenting lessons my mother and father implanted in my heart. Those ideas are nothing new or radical, just logical and effective.

One evidence of positive, not perfect, parenting that they imparted to me is quite simple – I continue to wake up every morning anxious and excited to get on with another good day!

About the Author

I grew up in a small town of 59 people in the middle of the Adirondack Mountains of New York State.

Once I understood you don't have to be perfect to be successful, life became enjoyable. My parents taught me that doing the right thing at the right time produced positive results.

Mom and Dad both worked, but that did not prevent us from doing things as a family. We went camping, played neighborhood softball games, went to the drive-in theater for all the John Wayne movies, bowled together, and ate dinner (actually, we called it supper) together.

My independent actions and ideas were allowed, even encouraged. Buying amateur radio equipment or a new BB-gun gave me the opportunity to find a job to pay for it. Thus, raising chickens and selling the eggs, even picking and canning tomatoes for the lady down the road became part of my middle school years.

During the early years of college, my relationship with God gave me the courage to deal with some tough emotional challenges.

Now, as an experienced classroom teacher, parent and grand-parent, I am thankful for the parenting lessons my mother and father implanted in my heart. Those ideas are nothing new or radical, just logical and effective.

One evidence of positive, not perfect, parenting that they imparted to me is quite simple – I continue to wake up every morning anxious and excited to get on with another good day!

Read more at https://johnhitchcockauthor.com.